Horse Breeds

Cara Krenn

Lerner Publications ◆ Minneapolis

For Kelly

Lerner Publications Company
An imprint of Lerner Publishing Group, Inc.
241 First Avenue North
Minneapolis, MN 55401 USA

For reading levels and more information, look up this title at www.lernerbooks.com.

Main body text set in Billy Infant Regular. Typeface provided by SparkType.

Editor: Nicole Berglund

Library of Congress Cataloging-in-Publication Data

Names: Krenn, Cara, author.
Title: Horse breeds / Cara Krenn.
Description: Minneapolis : Lerner Publications, [2025] | Series: Lightning bolt books ® - horse lover's library | Includes bibliographical references and index. | Audience: Ages 6-9 | Audience: Grades 2-3 | Summary: "There are so many horse breeds to explore! Curious readers will enjoy learning about types of heavy horses, light horses, and ponies"—Provided by publisher.
Identifiers: LCCN 2023035412 (print) | LCCN 2023035413 (ebook) | ISBN 9798765626054 (library binding) | ISBN 9798765628898 (paperback) | ISBN 9798765634882 (epub)
Subjects: LCSH: Horse breeds—Juvenile literature. | Horses—Juvenile literature.
Classification: LCC SF291 .K74 2025 (print) | LCC SF291 (ebook) | DDC 636.1—dc23/eng/20230728

LC record available at https://lccn.loc.gov/2023035412
LC ebook record available at https://lccn.loc.gov/2023035413

Manufactured in the United States of America
1-1009870-51939-9/19/2023

Table of Contents

What Is a Horse Breed?

And they're off! Horses burst through the starting gates and speed down the track.

Some horses are built to run fast. Others are bigger and slower.

A Clydesdale horse stands in front of a Shetland pony.

A girl learns how to ride a horse.

Over time, people have raised horses with features they like. A group of horses with certain features is called a breed.

There are hundreds of horse breeds. They have many different coat colors and patterns.

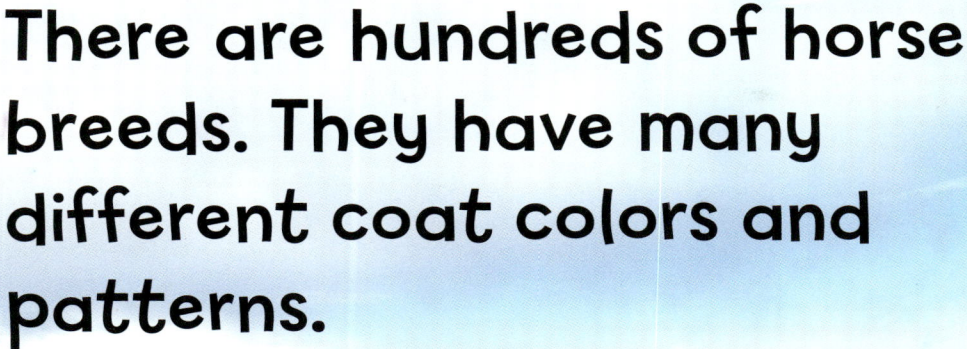

Heavy Horses

Heavy horses are very strong. They have big bodies, big hooves, and powerful legs.

Percherons are friendly and pretty. They pull carts for parades and hayrides.

Percherons pull a sleigh through the snow.

The shire is the world's biggest horse. It can weigh more than 2,000 pounds (908 kg)!

A woman stands with two shires.

Clydesdales take big steps with their huge hooves.

Clydesdales are famous for pulling wagons. They are hard workers.

Light Horses

Light horses are great for riding and racing. They are very fast.

Light horses have long legs and necks.

Thoroughbreds are superathletes! These speedy horses run races.

Arabians are one of the oldest breeds. They have high tails, big eyes, and rounded faces.

Arabians can run 100-mile (161 km) races.

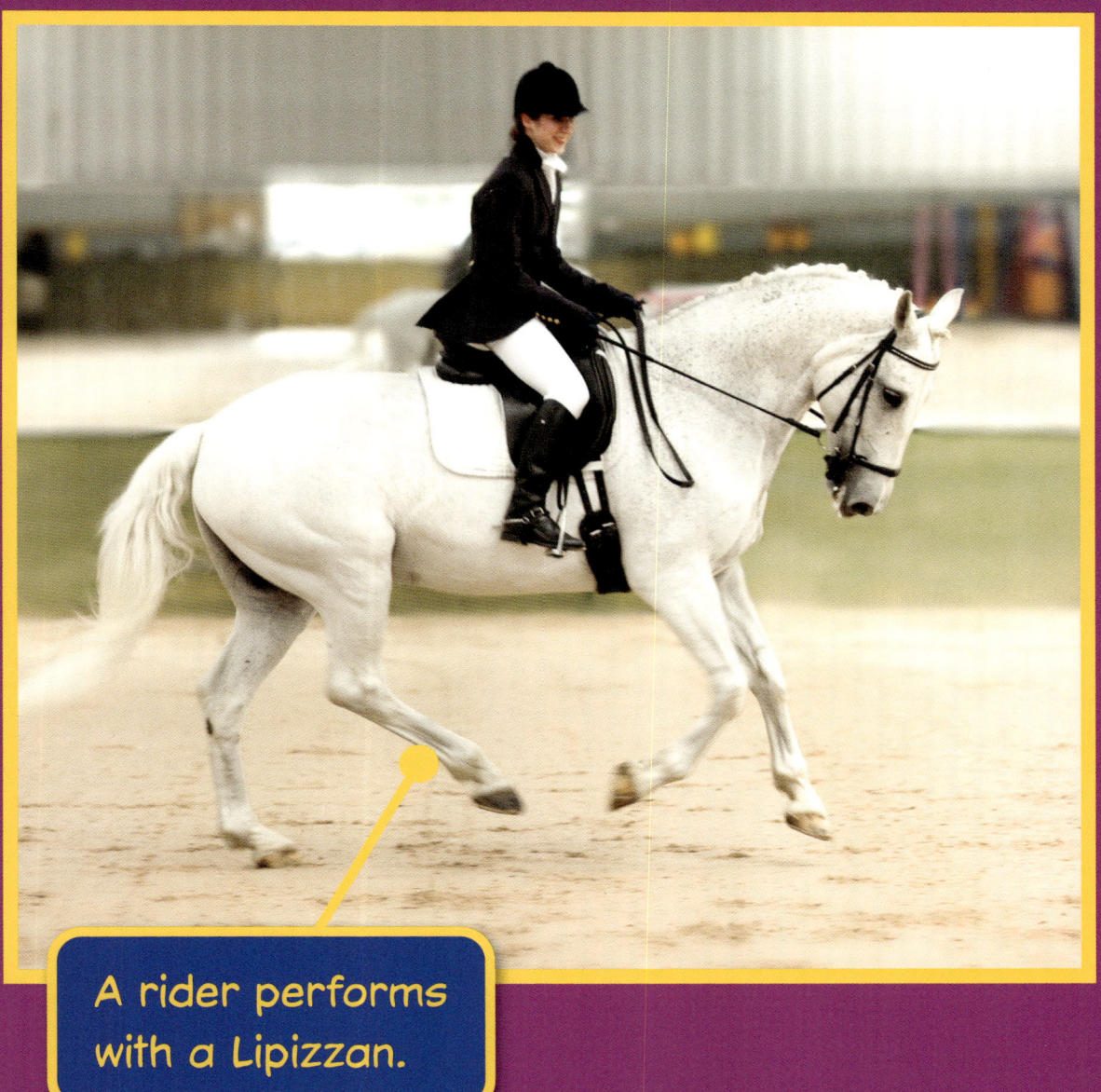

A rider performs with a Lipizzan.

Lipizzans can dance. They perform dressage, a special riding style.

Ponies

Ponies are small but mighty. They are good horses for kids to ride.

Shetland ponies were once used to carry things. They can pull loads below 90 pounds (41 kg).

All ponies are shorter than 58 inches (147 cm).

Spots make the Pony of the Americas special. It also has striped hooves.

A Pony of the Americas walks in a field.

From big horses to small ponies, horses come in all shapes and sizes. Each one is special in its own way!

A girl brushes her horse.

Horse Breeds and You

Different breeds do different jobs. Which breed is your favorite?

Fun Facts

- Clydesdale hooves are the size of dinner plates.

- Thoroughbreds can run about 40 miles (65 km) per hour.

- Shetland ponies eat grass, blackberries, and even seaweed!

Glossary

breed: a group of horses that share certain features

coat: hair on an animal's body

dressage: a riding style in which horses are trained to perform special moves

feature: traits of an animal, such as coat color

hoof: curved horn that protects the foot of a horse

race: to compete to be the fastest

Learn More

American Museum of Natural History: All about Horses
https://www.amnh.org/explore/ology/zoology/all-about-horses

Barder, Gemma. *Be a Horse and Pony Expert*. New York: Crabtree, 2021.

Britannica Kids: Horse
https://kids.britannica.com/kids/article/horse/353265

Grack, Rachel. *Race Horses*. Minneapolis: Jump!, 2024

Idzikowski, Lisa. *Horse Sports*. Minneapolis: Lerner Publications, 2025.

Kiddle: Horse Facts for Kids
https://kids.kiddle.co/Horse

Index

Photo Acknowledgments

Image credits: gabriel12/Shutterstock, p. 4; Thinkstock/Getty Images, p. 5; Caia Image/ Getty Images, p. 6; Michael Roberts/Getty Images, p. 7; vikarus/Getty Images, p. 8; THEPALMER/Getty Images, p. 9; intst/Getty Images, p. 10; Gannet77/Getty Images, p. 11; MV Photo/Getty Images, p. 12; Bloomberg/Getty Images, p. 13; Westend61/Getty Images, pp. 14, 20; Tim Platt/Getty Images, p. 15; JTSorrell/Getty Images, p. 16; Kevin Schafer/Getty Images, pp. 17, 20; Carina Maiwald/Alamy, p. 18; KuznetsovDmitry/Getty Images, p. 19.

Cover Dan Baillie / 500px/Getty Images.